Growing Readers

Purchased with Smart Start Funds

# Brothers

by Lola M. Schaefer

Consulting Editor: Gail Saunders-Smith, Ph.D.

Consultant: Phyllis Edelbrock, First-Grade Teacher,
University Place School District, Washington

Pebble Books

an imprint of Capstone Press
Mankato, Minnesota

1

Pebble Books are published by Capstone Press
818 North Willow Street, Mankato, Minnesota 56001
http://www.capstone-press.com

*Library of Congress Cataloging-in-Publication Data*
Schaefer, Lola M., 1950–
     Brothers/by Lola M. Schaefer.
     p. cm.—(Families)
     Includes bibliographical references and index.
     Summary: Simple text and photographs depict brothers and what they can do
with each other.
     ISBN 0-7368-0253-3
     1. Brothers—Juvenile literature. [1. Brothers.] I. Title. II. Series: Schaefer, Lola M.,
1950–   Families.
HQ759.96.S32   1999
306.875′2—dc21                                                                                    98-45158
                                                                                                          CIP
                                                                                                          AC

# Note to Parents and Teachers

The Families series supports national social studies standards for
units related to identifying family members and their roles in the
family. This book describes and illustrates brothers and activities
they do with each other. The photographs support emergent readers
in understanding the text. The repetition of words and phrases
helps emergent readers learn new words. This book also introduces
emergent readers to subject-specific vocabulary words, which are
defined in the Words to Know section. Emergent readers may need
assistance to read some words and to use the Table of Contents,
Words to Know, Read More, Internet Sites, and Index/Word List
sections of the book.

# Table of Contents

4

Brothers can have sisters.

Brothers can have brothers.

8

Brothers can be twins.

Brothers feed the dog.

Brothers play the piano.

Brothers go fishing.

Brothers play in
tree houses.

Brothers blow bubbles.

Brothers can be
best friends.

# Words to Know

**brother**—a boy or man who has the same parents as another person

**piano**—a large musical instrument with black keys and white keys; people press the keys to make music.

**sister**—a girl or woman who has the same parents as another person

**tree house**—a playhouse made among the branches of a tree

**twins**—two children born at the same time to the same parents; some twins look the same and some twins look different.

# Read More

**Bailey, Debbie.** *Brothers.* North York, Ont., Canada: Annick Press, 1993.

**Gans, Lydia.** *Sisters, Brothers, and Disability: A Family Album.* Minneapolis: Fairview Press, 1997.

**Saunders-Smith, Gail.** *Families.* People. Mankato, Minn.: Pebble Books, 1998.

**Skutch, Robert.** *Who's in a Family?* Berkeley, Calif.: Tricycle Press, 1995.

# Internet Sites

**Family.com**
http://family.go.com

**The Family Fun Network—Kids Room**
http://www.ffn.org/kids.htm

**Just 4 Kids**
http://www.herald.ns.ca/news/kids.html

# Index/Word List

best, 21
blow, 19
brothers, 5, 7, 9, 11, 13, 15, 17, 19, 21
bubbles, 19
can, 5, 7, 9, 21
dog, 11
feed, 11
fishing, 15

friends, 21
go, 15
have, 5, 7
piano, 13
play, 13, 17
sisters, 5
tree houses, 17
twins, 9

## Word Count: 36
## Early-Intervention Level: 4

**Editorial Credits**
Mari C. Schuh, editor; Steve Weil/Tandem Design, cover designer and illustrator; Kimberly Danger, photo researcher

**Photo Credits**
David F. Clobes, 10, 12, 18
Dennie Cody/FPG International LLC, 6
Diane Meyer, 8
International Stock/Roger Markham, cover
Oscar C. Williams, 1, 4
Unicorn Stock Photos/Eric R. Berndt, 14, 16
Uniphoto/Mitch Diamond, 20

Special thanks to Joy Allison, Lori Hollenback, and Penny McCarthy, first-grade teachers at Evergreen Primary in University Place, Washington, for reviewing the books in the Families series.